REESE LIEBERMAN

living
proof

poems and prose

Also by Reese Lieberman

this world from my 2 eyez

Unmistakably Human

living proof

poems and prose

Reese Lieberman

to the past, for stepping out of the way & enabling us to move forward, & for guiding us into all of our tomorrows

& for anyone who needs proof that things will be alright, this is for you.

TABLE OF CONTENTS

Introduction

Poetry is looking at life through a magnifying glass. That is exactly what I wanted to do in this collection of poetry. Some of these poems tell stories, some explore those moments where you can't help but think to yourself, "Wow, I'm so lucky to be alive." It is somewhere between pure nonfiction and unhindered imagination. Some zoom in on momentary feelings, but then again, they're all fleeting aren't they? Therefore I wanted to write about things that may not be considered noteworthy. Because it's all a part of the human experience and that's what this book is about. I wrote these poems at the highs, the lows, and everything in between. There have been moments in life when I didn't know how to move forward, or if it was possible. Days in which tomorrow was hard to see. I wrote these poems with tired hands and a smile tugging at my cheeks, through teary-eyed moments, and with a clear mind retrospectively.

Living proof is remembering how you got this far. It is looking to the past to put trust in the future. It is a collection of poems, or more accurately, glimpses of life under a magnifying glass. It is reminders that we survived. Every time that we thought we wouldn't, we did.

And if ever there was proof that we can make it to tomorrow, it's that we made it through yesterday. This is a book I needed to read just as much as I needed to write. It is progress. It is documentation.

I am living proof. This book is living proof, and so, my friend, are you.

xx
Reese Lieberman

"I am out with lanterns looking for myself."

Emily Dickinson

"Most of what I know,
I learned from falling and getting back up.

The ground has taught me more about flight than
the sky ever could."

Rudy Francisco

A note from the author

Life can look a lot of ways, and *living proof* is how mine looks at this stage. I know it won't always be this way, I am constantly evolving, my life is forever changing. That is precisely why I put it down in ink.

living proof

scars & chapped lips
tan lines & dark under eyes
remind me that I've lived

spring tides & fleeting highs
the rise & fall of my chest
bring to light that I'm alive

the fading of my mind into rest,
the subtle awareness
that I am but a guest,
this heart, this soul, this poem,
all of this, my friend —
is living proof that I can do it again

Reese Lieberman

I Wasn't Built for Winter

I was born in December
but I wasn't made for Winter,
freezing beneath this sweater.
I was born & raised in
the mountains
but altitude is foreign to me now.
Funny how we lose our accents,
our ambitions & our innocence
but it's all still there in a more
real sense
deep down somehow.

I was born in the cold
& now look at me,
wrapped tightly in a long coat
so I don't freeze.
Southern Octobers
make me shiver.
You see, I wear my heart
on my sleeve
that's why I wasn't built
for Winter

spring rain

the rain falls down,
it's only down from here
and yet it is so sweet
a harmonic symphony,
fingers intertwined with sunshine,
a kaleidoscopic love,
electric touch
& i am revived,
i feel my heart beating
& i am reminded of this sweet,
sweet life
as the raindrops descend
upon my face
spring is on the tip of my tongue,
not a hint of bitter aftertaste,
so little time yet so much grace

overlooked

they say this type of love and exquisite joy doesn't exist, but i find it every day in places they sorely miss. i find it in the trees brandishing their october leaves above my head. i find it in the special eclipse of sunshine that comes in the moments when rain falls yet doesn't pour, and the clouds part just enough to let the rays illuminate the droplets. i find it in guitar strings, sweet melodies, tragic undertones. i find it in rolling the windows down on back roads, breeze in my face as the radio plays. i find it in the butterfly fluttering just inches away. i find it in morning teas and interlaced fingers, in the rhythmic redundancy of baking that becomes habitual, almost a reflex, & the sweet scent that lingers. in pen and paper, the pressure that is alleviated by the presence of an eraser. the ease that comes with gentle laughter. comfortable silence and deep conversations. they say this type of love, this type of joy doesn't exist, but it's staring them in the face, begging to be noticed.

i miss you but i've grown

i miss you like the sweet summertime misses
spring / like the moon misses her love, the darling
sun / i miss you so very much / but i miss you like a
goodbye i don't want to split in two / i miss you but
there are just some things i've got to do and places
i've got to be / i miss you but you can't take a part of
me / because darling once i felt safe with you, my soul
recognized yours as home / but now i look at you and
i'm reminded of a well-loved dress i've outgrown.

I want to grow a garden

I want to grow a garden / what I mean is, I want to be ever in the presence of life. / I want to soak up every possible ounce of sunlight. / I want to care for things with my bare hands. / I want to be gentle, and I want to be treated as such. / I want to put just the right amount of water into flowerpots. / I want to watch things grow. / I myself want to grow. / To watch my leaves turn from brown to gold. / My petals have been folded for far too long, I want to bloom. / I want to be one of those people who walks into a room and makes others feel unafraid to be themselves. / I want to be a gardener. / What I mean is, I want to take better care of myself. / To nurture myself until I grow to my full potential. / I want no longer to carry this armor I have shaped around my heart. / You see, all this time I've been trying to fix things that don't need to be fixed. / They need to be nourished. / They need to heal. / I have fallen in love with so very many people and places and things, it's time I love myself too. / I want to feel alive again. / To be a person ladybugs land on. / And so I must nourish the fruits and flowers and trees within me. / When I say I want to grow a garden, this is what I mean. //

Poetry Knows Everything

If I am
a ball of yarn
tightly wrapped,
hard to read

      poetry is
   the fingers
     unraveling me

 watch me turn from
 a tight knot

     to a loose   string

     because poetry
   knows everything

the rain taught me to let go

despite how it hurt me, still i could never bring
myself to hate the rain.
i knew that some part of it was healing me,
even when all it did was cause me pain.
i can't tell you the origin of this bittersweet love,
but i can tell you this; when the skies are rough
edges bleeding out i can feel a mirrored action
in my veins.
i am breathless, mesmerized by the largeness of it
all, the smallness of the droplets that fall.
& i am only myself, washed away of the things
i am not.
& it pierces through me in moments like this
that i don't have to carry baggage that i haven't
even really got.

one morning i awoke

one morning i woke up, not expecting anything from the day.

but quite on the contrary, pondering what i might bring to the day.

i chose to be myself. spirit & soul, in either hand. heart so brilliantly uncaged & thriving, to its own beat that wouldn't exist if it weren't for every other tune, on my sleeve.

one morning i awoke, eyes wide wanting only to savor every glimpse of this wonderful, beautiful moment of a life.

on that day i set out to do only one thing; to live every moment to the best of my ability. to try my very best, & i promised that that would be enough for me.

& guess what? i did it. i lived.

i soaked in the sunshine, i waltzed in the rain.

my smile spoke the loudest, but then so did my pain.

i felt joy & i knew sorrow, i was an old friend of yesterday & a stranger to tomorrow.

it was the same as every other day, if that is possible.

only i myself was different.

one morning i woke up & nothing was the same
except for everything.

remember me

remember me as a summer breeze.
lemonade on a hot day, i'll be the lemon whenever
you need & i'll be the hands that squeeze out its
sour juice, mixing it with sugar & water, turning it
into something sweet.
remember me as the words "i love you" scribbled
on a sticky note.
the shoulder that allows you to lean on it despite its
soreness.
remember me for late nights when you need
company.
remember me for letting the moment pass rather
than holding on to pettiness, please.
remember me for wanting a slice of your fruit or
a french fry off your plate & always sharing mine.
remember me for making you laugh when tension
hangs in the air.
remember me for lending you my jacket & not
mentioning it when you didn't return it.
remember me for baking for you, not because i have
to but because i want to.
remember me for the way i listen, noticing what
makes your eyes light up & listening more intently.
remember me for writing poems about you.
remember me for giving the tightest hugs.
remember me for never being scared to say those
precious & nonetheless plentiful three words.
remember me for sending you videos of songs that
made me think of you. remember me for carrying
the groceries so you don't have to.

if you're going to remember me, forget all of the above and remember me for just one thing; the way i loved.

Beautiful Ache

All this time you've
been aching to be beautiful
I can't help but wonder
why you can't see
that you already are

maybe it's because
all the products they sell
on the beauty aisle shelves
promise to make you
a star

maybe it's codependency,
a toxic relationship
between you and your
deepest insecurities

maybe it's because
you forgot who you were
before you became what
they told you to be

maybe it's because
as long as you're pretending
and pretending turns
to lies
there can never be peace
between your body,
soul and mind

maybe it's because
you believed what
they told you
and bought what they
sold you

maybe it's because
nothing is natural these days
and all they seem to care
about are artificial
hair dyes and skinny waists

maybe it's because
when you were a child
they told you to stop
being so wild,
replaced your running shoes
with a dress
they must've forgotten
the symbiosis between
a kid and their mess
maybe it's because
you internalized every
hateful comment
you ever heard
or maybe it started with
two simple words,
"she's prettier"

maybe in a world like this
it hurts less to be fake
than to live with a beautiful
ache

Sea Glass

I am sea glass
broken down & beaten
into something beautiful,
luminescent, even enviable.
All my jagged flaws
smooth.
All my sharp edges curve,
but when I look
in the mirror
I know only one thing
for sure,
I will never be
that girl.

this

it's spring but summertime heat is settling in & making itself at home already / we kick our feet in the clear blue waters of a swimming pool / string lights illuminate our cheeks, golden from the may sun / thunder bears its teeth & we run / but all the while we laugh & chatter / as lightning shatters & we're back home / home, what a lovely word when it means something equally as lovely / still we continue to laugh & chatter / & it occurs to me in this moment that this, *this* is what really matters.

a softer light

we measure our lives in brimming
cups of tea,
there is a glimmer of the
marvelous hidden in the monotony,
interwoven like stars in
the dark & heavy quilt of night
the way it warms our bellies
like the dwindling embers of a fireplace
but without the sting

we measure our days in the outpouring
of birdsong
hope personified by those melodic
harmonies
fresh as an evening breeze,
sweet as summertime strawberries

we measure ourselves in smiles
& winks
fleeting, fickle little things
however momentary
because we are neither finite
nor infinite
we contain multitudes
we will always be plural
sentences that remain unfinished,
only commas & semicolons
but never, ever periods
always lowercase
because we ourselves are poetry
taking place

Bury the Fruits

You can take away
the leaves, the vines,
the branches
scavenge the soot,
bury the fruits
but you can't take the roots.

finding harmony

i want to slow down for a change
i seek adventure & avoid peace
but now i'm finally starting to see
my heart craves serenity
to be in touch with the world
around me
i hardly notice the brightening shades
of the leaves
the raindrops on my eyelids
busy filling the world with my own voice
i've forgotten the power that silence holds

listen. i am listening now.
there is so much music in this world
& my body is in tune, humming along
only my mind has resisted
but i finally see
my heart craves harmony

fruit for two

though i do love
the sweet taste of
bright strawberries
on a spring afternoon
or watermelon on a hot
summer evening
clementines will always be
my favorite fruit
because on the outside
they are orange
like the evening sun
but tough like the surface
of an unsmoothed stone
yet when you pull back
the layers of that rough peel,
the inside is soft & sweet
divided into slices
ready to eat
& in that way it reminds me
of you —
hard on the outside
but divinely gentle & pleasant
on the inside,
bursting with love
like rain into a gutter,
it pours into every little thing
that you do
& after all, my favorite fruit
was made for two

stars & seeds

my favorite poems always involve
the stars.
stars or something involving seeds,
preferably fruit.
perhaps they remind me of my own
smallness & the infinity within
these hands, this heart, this honey
colored soul.
they remind me that contradictions
can live within one being,
that in a lot of ways, everything
is a paradox
& that it can be beautiful even so.
& most of all, it can survive or
help others to.
so vast yet so frighteningly small
yet when i am gazing at the stars
or pulling back the peel of an orange,
none of it feels frightening at all.

sun kissed

the sun reaches out,
lending a bit of its shine
to my soul & my complexion
adorning my hair with golden streaks
& warming my blushing cheeks.
summer is in the air,
i can feel it in my bones, in my knees,
in my feet —
& the way they so long to run free.

another chance

I ate a cherry plum, it was that fresh kind of sweet. / I didn't even know cherry plums existed until a couple of days ago. / I dove into the waters headfirst, midsummer heat. / You reached for my hand — or did I reach for yours, my friend? / I laughed until my stomach ached the other day — I didn't think I'd feel that way again. / all this to say, I didn't realize how I'd been living until I caught a glimpse of how I *could* be living. / now life tastes like that fresh kind of sweet. / like summer days, strawberries, and peaches. / getting caught in a rainstorm but deciding to dance. / who knew what could come of giving happiness another chance? //

for the petals

my heart is open / my skin isn't tough despite being touched by thorns / I still see the roses for their petals / I still see the kitchens for their kettles / I still see the sticks & stones for where they're from / & the burns on my cheeks for the sun / because even though sticks & stones may break my bones they're still just rocks & they still used to be a part of something much greater than me / & if my heart isn't open, how could my eyes possibly see? //

Periphery of Spring

A monarch butterfly
& dozens of honeybees
gather at the periphery
of spring, the color of a cardinal's
ruffled wing
a nest of wasps join the dance,
I do not make a sound –
I do not dare disturb such peace
I hear birds chatter, I feel
my own heartbeat
A light breeze pirouettes
through my hair
& in this moment life is just
as it has always been
& in some inexplicable way,
I am whole again

let in good things

i'll never forget the feel of the breeze
on my face
or the sweetness of the ripe clementine
between my teeth
i didn't make it to today just to pass up
an opportunity,
i didn't make it to today just to rely on
the conception that tomorrow will take me

i'm here right now
the breeze on my face
clementine in my teeth
sometimes it's simple things like this
that allow one to let down their guard
and let in good things
right now i am surrendering
sometimes gratitude looks a lot like
remembering

this too shall pass

I know I won't feel this forever
all things pass
and I too am just passing through
on these crashing waves
teardrops make their way
avalanches down the mountains
of my face
but I know I won't feel this forever
this too shall pass
in the wake of something better

the world was kinder

I wished the world was kinder
so I told a stranger she was
beautiful / I held the door &
waved / I let the beetles walk
on by / the lizards sunbathed
& I made my path just a little
wider so as not to disturb
them / I wished the world was
just a little kinder & on that
day, it was //

altitude/attitude

I can't wait for the day you realize
it was worth weathering the storm,
every "wrong turn" led you here,
you had it in you, the strength
to make it through
from the very moment you were born
none of those moments
were for nothing, dear
please join me, it's a lovely view
looking at life for what you've become,
not what it's done to you

equilibrium

i'm in my grandmother's kitchen
we are making pizza (her version)
she tells me to spoon on the red sauce
& spread it out to the edges of the crust
don't add too much or you will ruin it,
don't add too little or it will be dry
& i begin to wonder if i will
ever be able to live my life like that —
enough but not too much
i've always been one to pour so much love
it oversaturates hearts
yet when i don't text they wonder
why they haven't heard from me
can moderation & abundance be achieved
simultaneously?
i wonder if i can ever be enough
without being too much
or if i will always be the type of person
to overwater plants
or leave them to shrivel in the sunshine
i wonder
        i wonder -
                i wonder -
but now my grandmother is speaking
to me, so i stop all the wondering
& pour on some cheese

titles

some people know the title
to every song
others can't quite place it
but could hum along
to every note
i'd like to be the type
who may forget titles
but knows the harmony
by heart
which is to say that
some love unwaveringly
& others memorize titles
& love to play a part

brutalized but never beaten

thunder cracks porcelain skies
followed by an entourage of lightning,
& still the skies refuse to break
the very plates of the earth shift
in a chaotic & continuous motion
& still the ground is firm as can be
tornadoes barrel through,
volcanoes erupt
tsunamis morph into a mountainous
flood,
wars are waged by men,
fought with guns, fought with bombs,
fought with gasses, fought like silly men
in castles, fought with various tactics —
moreover remorseless actions
& still, still this world will not be
broken, it may shake it will not shatter,
will not be beaten to nothing
thought it may quake
because this world refuses to break.

rare

you hold my dreams in the palm of your hand & i never realized how fragile they were until you touched them so gently. in that moment i could picture you in a flower shop, all the flowers you would nurture blossoming wildly. it was a beautiful sight, you smiled politely & it was just like that that you held my dreams — a flower vase to be treated with utmost care. & you remind me to water these wildflowers of mine before they wilt beyond repair. i don't know how or where your hands become so soft in such a sharp world but they come back to life in your presence. i know that now, i am lucky & this, this is rare.

Sandcastle

one mistake and i watch any semblance
of progress i made crumble away
every sand grain that took a bulldozer to move
circles the drain

Maybe Then

I want to pry the skin off of my bones / lie in the grass
& let the worms have at my insides / until I become
a part of something better / maybe then I'll feel alive
/ maybe then I'll be as I'm meant to be / maybe once
my flesh has become acquainted with this world I'll
be able to sit in the sun without cursing my skin or
my stomach or my thighs or my hair or my hips or
my mind / maybe once the ants & the roaches have
had their way with me / maybe then / when I am
indiscernible from the soil, wound tightly round the
roots of a tree / maybe then when I am foreign even to
myself / on the precipice of something great, maybe
then I'll allow myself to begin to believe that perhaps
there could be something minor bearing resemblance
to greatness within me. / maybe when a sunflower
comes to suck up all that is good in me & leave out the
rest / maybe then I'll feel better / maybe then I'll get
some rest / or maybe then I'll feel used & discarded
/ maybe when I finally get everything I wanted I'll
realize there was just one thing I disregarded / in
trying to heal myself I have become an open wound
/ in trying to fix myself, I have broken more pieces
than I'd like to acknowledge / I could've dodged the

bullet, but instead it looks like I'm the one who shot it / left to collect the pieces / only to realize in the end, sometimes there are things in life that are impossible for a reason. //

Things Even Time Can't Take

We laugh so hard our muscles ache
& it occurs to me that there are
some things even time can't take,
some moments lived so loudly
their echoes will always remain
because these moments aren't just
memories, they are pieces of us
that won't fade
no matter how much the world
around us may change.

Reese Lieberman

The sun emerged & I made up my mind

On a hot Summer day
love taught me patience,
a stranger was kind,
the breeze tousled my hair,
a cardinal flew by
in a brilliant blur,
I got tired of waiting,
the sun emerged
& I made up my mind —

I'm shedding this hardness
that has grown around my heart
in the Winter
& Spring couldn't ease.
My soul aches for softness,
for kindness, for love
& so I have come to the
conclusion that I will become it
in time.

it's been raining less

i wake to the soft sound of birdsong
outside my bedroom rather than
the startling blare of my alarms
writing has become more about the words
and less about the word count i'm at
there's finally color in my cheeks again
and tan lines on my arms
it's been raining less since i stopped
looking at the forecast
i nearly forgot what it's like to gaze up
at the stars, but it's been raining less
and i'm finding answers to questions
i didn't know i needed to ask

Reese Lieberman

To Be at Peace

The only way to true happiness
is peace,
is knowing oneself
I am nothing more,
nothing less
than the oxygen I breathe;
just as this great, diligent tree
that rises far above my head
I stand at the base of it,
gray bark & an abundance of vines
upon which my shoulder rests.
To be in this moment,
feet on the ground,
eyes on the skyline,
is to be at peace.
I am nothing more,
nothing less
than this heartbeat
& what is that if not a wonderful
relief?

Wilting Leaves

You don't stop watering
a garden just because it is
not growing as quickly
as you'd like,
in fact wilting leaves
are nothing short of screams —
you see, it is all the more
reason to lend it what
it needs

Summer's Sweet

The scent of clementines
& freshly brewed tea.
Early morning settles into
our eyes.

If I could I'd bottle up
this feeling
or put it into song &
play it on repeat.

Strawberries & sunsets,
this Summer's sweet
cotton candy clouds
& seeds between my teeth.

There's nowhere else
I'd rather be
& I think that's what it is
to be genuinely happy & at peace.

The Woodpecker

First I hear the tap, tap, tapping
of the beak
not a moment later I see
a dusting of wood falling,
swept up in a breeze
but pulled down by its own weight
& gravity.
Then I notice the striking crimson
that adorns its head —
the woodpecker above me
in a tree
& in that moment I am reminded
of that which I have forgotten
yet innately know,
life is so much larger than it
seemed
a moment ago.

Patient Being

Sing me a song, teach me a verse,
I whispered to the wind
when all it ever wanted was
to be heard.
Sometimes silence is the only
solution, but I'm not nearly as quiet
as I should be.
But then I walk into the woods,
lips sealed & I am reminded
of all the many things that I could be.
I'm not quite sure if it's more
frustrating or freeing —
if only I were
              a more patient being.

The Leaves Have Fallen

Soon the trees will be bare
& the weather touched with
cold & bitter
I've been thinking maybe
it's time I cut my hair.
The trees are beginning to
lose their leaves
& I envy them.
There are so many things I
wish I could let go of as
easily as they do.

Reese Lieberman

At My Feet

One morning I went for a walk,
a quarter past ten.
It was nothing out of the ordinary
but then I nearly stepped on a caterpillar
thinking it was a branch or a twig,
already disassembled from its life force—
not a life force of its own,
only the beginning of a beautiful story.

I watched as it hurried along the
pavement, coiling & uncoiling
its mossy green body.
Since then, my footsteps have been lighter,
I more carefully eye where my foot falls
for you never know what may be on
the pavement in the sunshine making
its own way across the street.
Be gentle with the universe—
sometimes it is at your very feet.

petrichor

I want to be like the Earth
after it rains
wet dirt in my veins
flowers opening after
night ends
hours soaked now to feel
light again
blooming in the rich petrichor
gray skies looming no more
I want to be like the Earth
after it rains
fresh dirt in my veins

Reese Lieberman

An ode to the human heart

The human heart is so small yet
so infinitely large all at once.
Pumping gallon after gallon daily,
aorta opening up, letting out blood.
Even intricacies seem less
delicate when you consider
the sheer strength of the muscle
that beats & beats & beats
all for the sake of life—
or quite possibly love.

The human heart has a limitless
capacity for love,
if only we open ourselves up to it,
like a sunflower to the sun
perhaps that's what's most impressive:
how something so small
could have love for so very much
in a universe mind bendingly
vaster than the mind can
comprehend.

The human body has 60,000
miles of blood vessels in it—
that's twice the circumference
of the earth inside of you,
all leading back to the heart.
They say nobody knows the reason why
the heart is associated with love,
well I can find a few
but perhaps that's just it—
love needn't be comprehensible.

A Promise

Fall comes with a promise,
one I ache to keep
it includes but is not limited to:
clearing up these bags beneath
my eyes that want for sleep,
using these legs that are ready
to run, fulfilling the wish of these
cheeks to be kissed by the sun,
nurturing my body with a hot cup
of tea & my mind with the
paperbacks on my wooden shelf.
Fall comes with a promise,
not to the trees or the changing
leaves, not even to the weather,
or good health— but to myself.

Reese Lieberman

What's Done Is Done

What's done is done,
but if I'm not mistaken
the sun rose today
the planets revolved,
earth, our beloved home,
spun on its axis.
What's done is done,
but if I'm not mistaken
stardust & empty space
are at the center of
everything we know
& tonight the sun
will set
not all so that you can
sit here
wishing on stars that
you could turn time
backward.
What's done is done,
but if I'm not mistaken
after a storm shook up
its world
a cardinal found its way
home,
a snail crawled, in the
way snails do as though
in slow motion
& found its way too.

living proof

What's done is done,
but if I'm not mistaken
the earth is still orbiting
a sun that rose in a new day
that is unwritten
for me & for you.

I think of us

I think about us in the pouring rain / something about that particular shade of gray, the rhythmic patter of the droplets pulls us back to our roots / simpler versions of ourselves / you may look away from sunshine but rain will not be denied / on evenings like this, nature refuses to be ignored / slowly, our hearts recognize the familiar rhythm & syncopate to the rain / the rise & fall of our chests match the patterns of those vast curtains of gray / we are yet another f r a g m e n t of nature with stardust in our eyes & shoes full of water / beneath our veils of metaphors & tipping hats / on evenings like this, there's no denying that. //

While My Footprints Disappeared

The day passed by, I saw it as though in a rearview mirror. I chased it but it wouldn't be caught. The sun set with no great reluctance. The moon danced with the tides. I tried but failed to capture that moment, as though it were a crab that can be caught in a cup or a lizard that can be grabbed between fingers and palms. I tried so hard to save it that I did not savor it. The moon dipped into the horizon. Dusk came and went silently. The sun returned, carrying her warmth with her. Life, I'm sure, blossomed beneath the sea. All the while my footprints disappeared.

the future is heavy in my hands

it feels like my future was placed
in the palm of my hands
but I swear they're too small
to bear this weight,
what if making a choice means
making a mistake?
how long can a back carry this
baggage until it breaks?
time is a train I missed
I'm barefoot running to catch up
but it's weighing on me like lead.
excitement has turned to dread
maybe it's all in my head
but the future is a heavy thing to carry
around in the palm of your hand
time is full speed ahead,
I'm caught in quicksand
I feel terribly small when I think
about the future, it's far too vast
for me to navigate without a map,
but here I am, knowing that is
what I must do in the end.
I can't help but wonder
if fate will be a friend.

she was magic

her feet were always bare
the ground was mostly rough
& yet somehow
she managed to keep them soft

her fingertips had calluses & blisters
from all her hard work
& yet her touch remained gentle
unlike many who roam this earth

rarely was her voice heard
& yet she kept on singing

there was so much love
in her heart despite her hardships
that all her body could do
was mimic it

if i were the sun looking down
at her smile
i would wish desperately
that i could match it
she had that effect,
that can only be described as magic

but there was no magic,
the truth is *she was magic*

Reese Lieberman

I exist in fragments

I exist in fragments,
in the corners of my unmade bed,
in the lessons I've learned
& inked into the page
I exist in my messy penmanship
& handwritten letters
I exist in the lives around me
& the visible traces of my efforts
to be better
you can find me in my scribbled
notes & underlines in my
favorite books,
my blurry photographs of sunsets
& the product of my attempts
to cook something new
or the colorful laces I used to
replace the boring plain ones
in my shoes
I exist in that poem I wrote
once long ago about learning
to fly & growing wings
I exist in scattered pieces,
can't you see?

I exist because of these things.

[I Am] What Survives the Wreckage

Home is a pile of rubble / & I can feel the remnants sinking into my stomach. / Nothing survives that kind of wreckage & I can still feel myself there, amongst the remains. / A million moments pass all in one, but this is it, it's really done. / So why am I still holding onto nothing but dust riddled air when even that slips through my fingers? / All that once stood came crashing down but the memory still lingers. / If the chaos is all done, why am I still trying to make peace with it? / I am here in the wreckage trying to salvage even a piece of it / Given more time to reflect on it, will it feel less impossible? / 'Cause I just can't seem to let it go //

I've washed the scent out of all my clothes, but every now & then I catch a whiff of the stench in my nose. / It's funny the things that remind you of home / like leaking ceilings & fire alarm tones. / It's funny how quickly things get out of hand / Nothing survives that kind of wreckage, but here I am. //

Scars Are the Truth

Forever is bleeding
& we're just catching the drops
in our palms,
collecting scars as we chase
after stars.
Sometimes I think it's a wonder
how we got this far.
This world is a cruel place
for a keeper of an open heart;
but we won't betray ourselves,
so we've become well acquainted
with pain,
no bandages to show but
riddled with invisible aches.
Scars are the truth so we wear
them with pride
in a world that touts dishonesty
and urges us to hide—
we stand tall,
reaching out to our brethren.
Mine is yours and yours is mine.
Forever is bleeding
and we're just living our lives.

Becoming Reacquainted With Silence

You must know peace
before you can know yourself,
become reacquainted with silence
& sunrises
let moments pass in which you
aren't chasing anything but the stillness
in your own mind
only then can you know yourself
more than ever
only then can you grow into the marvelous
masterpiece you were destined
to become

rocking chair mind

my mother says i've got a rocking chair mind / writing out all the options, making so much trouble to decide / my mother says i should think less / my mind is too tightly wound with stress / my indecisiveness eats away at me / if i could i would make it all stop, trust me, i wouldn't be waiting / but how can i possibly turn it off when i've always had an overly active imagination? //

the sound of defiance

does honey's sweetness take the sting away from moments like this when it feels like the world is caving in? i think not but it's worth it anyway. don't you hear that? the sound of your heartbeat. that is the sound of defiance. that is the sound of your being. that is the sound that kept going despite the rushing tides that tried to silence what dares not to be silenced. i want to be like that. i want to be the flame that won't quit despite the downpour. despite the abundance of carbon dioxide and scarcity of oxygen. and don't forget—what is embers one moment the next may be a roaring flame.

Reese Lieberman

we are the universe

the tide will come in
and the tide will go out
what's mine for now will be yours
someday, somehow
we are the universe after all
summer has beckoned fall
lanterns illuminate the streets
it's pumpkin season, boots
become reacquainted with feet
the dead leaves kiss the soil,
soon to become one;
we fade into the night,
we are the setting sun

the ants

i stood beneath a tree. a great vast beautiful thing that felt miles bigger than me. a butterfly fluttered across my eyeline, landing on a leaf as green as a fern. a woodpecker chipped away creating a rhythmic sensation. a great big hawk landed at the very top. two smaller birds, mockingbirds perhaps, bullied it into flying away. i wondered why it let those birds squawk away in its face without making so much as a cry in return but then i suppose that's just a cycle of the world. i look down and i see the visible entanglement of the roots sprawled across the ground. an ant colony has made its home at the foot of this tree, something much larger and more complex than it may seem. even the ants seem to have a rhythm. there is purpose in everything they do. i doubt that we can all say the same, but then again perhaps we can. a breeze picks up, a coolness against my cheeks. a rustling in my hair. the tree is immovable. sometimes i wonder if my generation has roots. most of us don't like to be tied down. all we do is tie our shoes every morning so that our feet might take us somewhere new. but then i wonder if it isn't something deeper, and perhaps invisible in one sense but really quite the opposite in another. perhaps we are just like the ants.

the soles of my boots

the soles are falling off of my favorite boots / i
super glued them once, i'll super glue them again /
i wonder how broken they will have to be before i
realize that a little glue isn't enough to fix them. //

Drifting in the Crowd

Men on the street drink
until they are emptier than the bottles
they leave behind with a clink.
Trash cans are piled high
they say "out of sight, out of mind"
but I can see it all, miles high.
A mother chases after her
young daughter,
her hip occupied by a toddler.
A man rides by on a bicycle;
a skater's board breaks.
The world doesn't change,
nobody bats an eye,
nobody turns their face.
We're just a tide of strangers
in a familiar place.

I Finally Met Myself in the Green

I.

I think I finally met myself in the green
this evening,
I know it sounds crazy but just listen
before you don't believe me
I saw winding roots,
I saw spiny leaves,
I saw leisurely squirrels
& rushing streams
I stepped inside & got lost
within dreams
within dreams
I saw the most marvelous sights
& before you ask,
they are not what you think
in fact they were the most mundane
of things
I saw toothbrushes,
showers, & city lights
I saw dewdrops on flowers,
teapots, & kites

I saw stars—
the most mundane of all
the things that shine
unfailingly in the one thing
more promising than days—
night
yet they are the most magical sight
I have seen in all my life

II.

I kept trekking,
I saw winding roots,
I saw spiny leaves,
I saw leisurely squirrels
& rushing streams
I stepped inside & got lost
within dreams
within dreams
within me

I caught sight of my
own two footprints
I followed them like a dog on a sniffing trail
to see where they would lead—
they led me to the stars,
they stole away to the sea,
they took me down unfamiliar avenues
& up foreign streets
lastly, they led me straight
to my own front doorstep,
I pulled up the mat,
inscribed with one word "home"
& adorned with a heart,
in search of a key,
they left me with nothing—
            exactly what I need

III.

I finally met myself in the green
this evening,
if you know what I mean,
congratulations
& if you don't
    there's nothing left
    to say but
    grab a coat & a lantern
        & good luck.

A Frivolous Pastime

I'm trying to catch stardust
in my palm,
then it's there,
then it's gone.
All too quickly
for me to hold on.

These Words

These words will last
for longer than the hands
that write them,
this pen,
this pen will run dry
these pages,
these pages might tear,
might suffocate, might burn
for all I know
they might wind up in a landfill,
or labeled with a price tag
despite their apparent
lack of value
on a shelf in Goodwill
& even still
every now & again
as these words spill
from my landslide of a mouth
I can taste eternity in them,
I can taste forever, so I
spit them out

Afternoon Tea

Lately I've been feeling like
the kettle that boils my
afternoon tea—
like if I want to be heard
I must scream

Self Portrait in a Dream

My shadow followed me into
my dreams
I looked down at my reflection
in my sleep.
They say you aren't supposed
to be able to see these
sorts of things
but they found their way in,
they found their way in.

There were cracks in the mirror;
I tried to glue them all.
Raindrops splattered the canvas
that held my self portrait,
so I reached for an umbrella
but nothing I did seemed
to fix them
& I started to think that maybe
I shouldn't have let them in,
I shouldn't have let them in.

This umbrella's got holes
& this glue won't hold
there's cracks in my complexion
& raindrops making their way
into the crevices in my skin:
I let them in.

Nostalgia

Home is window shopping
at a closed-down strip mall.
A dream I wish I hadn't
woken from,
now I'll never know
how it ends.
Home is watching stars fall
on the television screen;
it has morphed from four walls
into every little memory,
every dream,
everything that we have
become &
all that we never will
be again.

Reese Lieberman

old dreams buried in my closet

out of reach, out of touch
a sweet dream but i just woke up
nothing but candle smoke
remnants & invisible things
old dreams buried deep within
my closet,
a stack of paper & a pair of wings
to me they were the best parts
of the universe that would
someday take me somewhere far,
to you they're inanimate objects
yet even time can't take the magic
out of stars
i've still got a photograph
of the cosmos somewhere that once
hung over my bed
they could always captivate me
in a way nothing else did
but now they're out of reach,
out of touch
a sweet dream but i just woke up

The World is Falling 2 Pieces

The world is falling to pieces,
the sky grows just a little darker
everyday
& my under eyes with it,
between the creases.
But I hear the sweet melody
of a bird,
the sun kisses my skin like
nothing else in this world.
I stand among living things,
vines & leaves & trunks
of trees,
much greater than me.
I listen to my favorite song
as I scribble down a poem
in my time-worn journal
& I savor the taste of an orange
that too has been kissed
by the sun.
My legs & my soul & my mind
thank me every time I run
& a kind stranger offered
to take our picture.
& I guess what I'm saying is,
for every broken piece
there is something bigger,
something better
which has assuredly made
it through rough weather
to be standing here now

as we all have.
& I guess what I'm saying is
despite all the woe & the
qualms & the bitterness,
there is reason to
be glad
you can lay down your
frustration & your heartache
& your anger
& just enjoy this moment.
the world will keep on
spinning
& besides it needs your light.
I guess what I'm saying is
the world may be falling
to pieces
but take a step outside
& I promise you, you will
find reason,
even in the night,
to carry on — a little
softer, a little sweeter —
in this life.

Tumultuous Sea

So we lie down
in the tumultuous
sea,
our skin opaque,
our eyes like weeds,

our hearts entangled.
You're a message
in a bottle,
I'm a sailor
befuddled.
You're words
on paper
in a language I never
learned to read.

You're a twilight
swim,
I'm a ship moored.
I'm lost on the
converging swells,
you're the crimson
shore.
I can't recall,
for the life of me,
what I set sail for.

The Light We Made Ourselves Into

Your eyes look golden in the sunlight,
as we walk across yellow street lines
painted by hands long ago
and far from sight.
Daffodils grow in unmowed grass
on the roadside.
A honeybee resides in the delicate
petals of one of the blossoms.
Just as the wild things,
we live so loudly that if our lives
become history it will be written in bold
with footnotes saying that we faced
this world unafraid,
unfazed by the shade
we ran towards the sun.
And if it could be said that we started
out as nothing but stardust and dew,
we will be proud of the light
we made ourselves into.

Dive in

Paint is meant to be splattered,
that lotion you've been saving in
your bathroom cabinet
is meant to soften your skin,
oranges were meant to be eaten,
your legs were meant to run,
your eyes were meant to see
the seasons,
the cadence of your laughter
was meant for fun.
Paint is meant to be splattered,
stop holding it in,
your life was meant to be lived;
who cares if your trousers
become torn or tattered?
What are you waiting for,
dive in.

life couldn't put your fire out

you're alive, you're alive
with the dirt & the trees
& the beetle & the soon
to be fallen leaves—
we all fall eventually
but it's not about
the plummet,
you're alive, you're alive
come lie in the dirt
with the trees & the beetles
& the leaves & me

remember when you
were a child collecting acorns
& running wild?
let's be like that again,
for we knew more
about everything
before we were taught
about anything

remember when all you knew
was your own two hands & feet
& the hunger in your belly
didn't come like thunder
you pull headphones over
your ears to block out?
do you remember trusting
the world?

living proof

when the skies poured,
we knew in our guts that
the sun would come back out
we didn't bother worrying
if the slides at the rusted playground
would hold our weight,
or if we were strong enough
to climb the monkey bars
but then we didn't worry at all,
for that matter, did we?

i'd like to get my
hands dirty again
won't you lie with me
in the soil, my friend?

i'm alive, i'm alive
i can feel it,
i survived

you're alive, you're alive
god knows life couldn't put
your fire out
though it sure tried

we're alive, we're alive
with the dirt & the trees
& the dust that collects
on memory & bookshelves
we're alive, we're alive
let's stop making strangers
of ourselves

come lie with me
among the beetles & the fallen leaves,
& the branches & the seeds

Big Heart

Her heart was too big to wear on her
sleeve: / it slipped through the space
between her lips when she smiled, /
the creases of her eyes, / the warmth
of her touch, / the sweetness of her
laughter. / Even her teardrops were
filled with love / she couldn't conceal
for she was so very full. / & that
is what made her breathtakingly
beautiful. //

This Ache Has No Manners

I've become so accustomed to this sweet, sweet ache
/ I feel it there, in the pit of my stomach / it is a song
caught on loop that I used to listen to in my   days of
youth / it is a summer afternoon reminiscent of those
long passed / it is the same sun, the same sky, the same
me only passing through a different fleeting moment
in time / it is being young but feeling so much older
than I was / it is these four walls I lie between / it is
looking around & realizing everyone around me has
changed / it is feeling sorry for those who haven't /
some might call it growing pains, but most days—
most days it lingers but bears no name //

fighting gravity

what do i do with the words caught
in my throat that will never escape? /
do i choke or do i drown? / or do i
just keep holding them down? /
fighting gravity is tiring / i can feel
my muscles expiring / my lower
lip bleeds from biting it so hard /
how am i to let go of this feeling
when it is holding onto me? /
crowding the space around my
heart / these words are strangling
me & all i know how to do is turn
them into art / while they slowly
tear me apart //

Vulnerability

I don't know how I feel
but I feel a lot
I feel naked
even when I'm not.
I feel myself bleeding
from phantom wounds.
It's all coming back to me
in screaming color,
the scars that had faded
are splitting in two.
I don't know how I feel
or what is true
all I know is that
I feel naked
even though I'm not.
The scars have faded
even though they're blue
& here I am, somewhere
I never thought I would be:
crying in front of you.

Said & Finally Done

I'd like to let these stories fade like echoes
into the background,
only pages not deserving a whole chapter
moments that do not define a character
a dusty piece of literature
I aspire to learn something from
not a mirror reflection of what is to come
but all that is said & finally done.
I shall welcome tomorrow with open arms,
today is a privilege to participate in
but I am glad those yesterdays are gone
which is to say, I am ready to move on.

i'm a matchstick

i have self-destructive tendencies
like losing sleep to the thought of you
like replaying all the bad moments
like making the same mistakes twice
like willfully unlearning the lesson
like letting you in again
like keeping all of it inside
like giving you everything
until there's nothing left of me
i'm a matchstick, do you know
how you burn right through me
without blinking an eye?
i'm down on my knees, you don't
even miss a beat, i give you all that's left
and all of my ashes too
i set my expectations too high
i accept too little
my flaws are winning the fight
i walk barefoot through life,
even when i know all too well
that some surfaces are far too rough for that,
& right now the ground is burning my feet
i try to run away, but i'm the fire
blazing my way through your gasoline

asking darkness for directions

I get so lost inside my head sometimes
I'm not anywhere at all
I'm not present nor gone
I'm not ready for the fall
I'm not anything at all
but I'm not nothing
if that counts for something
I'd like to be here for a while
leave this baggage at the door
and shake the stress off with a smile
my mind's been working over time
ever since I was a child
waiting for my life to begin
well this is life now, isn't it?
I get so lost inside my head
sometimes I'm not anywhere at all
but I don't want to miss this
I don't want to miss you
clinging to phantoms, begging
them to pull me through
asking darkness for directions
following the first stranger to
call out an answer, blindly
backtracking and wasting time
asking darkness for directions—
was light always this hard to find?

the 366th

i woke up this morning
& slipped into my shoes
they say not to make
the same mistake twice
but i've made this one
three hundred & sixty five
times & counting,
sometimes i wonder
if i'll ever escape it

but i woke up
this morning
& decided not to make it
the three hundred &
sixty sixth

returning to me

i am trying to forgive myself for all the
flaws you find in me / i am learning to
forget all the imperfections you taught
me to see / it's all become a bit clearer /
ever since i started remembering who
i was before you taught me what to see
when i look into the mirror //

searching for love

I miss the softness in life / dewdrops in the morning & watching the sunrise / I miss baking, creating something nourishing out of precise measurements & care / it's funny, this searching for love when all along it's been inside of me / I think it's time to open my heart & set it free. //

17

17 is a bitter discrepancy
everything and nothing like i dreamed it would be
17 is a one way street
all you want to do is get ahead while you fall so far
behind
18 feels like the starting line, definitive and
monumental
so why am i running a marathon if the race hasn't
even begun?
16 is a fever dream,
all i do is wax poetic
and dream of a life that hasn't quite started but is
already done
15 is a childhood home i can't go back to anymore
and i'm walking in circles
because 17 is one foot out the door

17 is a fly caught in a spider's web
everything makes more sense in my head
17 is unlearning every lesson only to learn it
the hard way again
i keep forgetting to grow towards the sun
because 17 is the dreadful in-between
you can't own anything and you can't pay rent
but you've got to rationalize your existence
17 is pool days and existential dread
achievements and regrets

17 is a balancing act
learning who's really got your back
when the people who bring you down are the ones
that should bring out the best in you
17 is wondering what happened to the rest of you
where is the light? where are the dreams?
17 is a million little screams

goodbye for now

september is starting to sweeten the air with the
likes of cinnamon and shifting seasons / autumn
feels significant, like i can hear the phrase "change
is inevitable" without a sense of dread in the pit of
my stomach / because i have seen that changes can
be good too /

i can feel the future drawing nearer but she will
answer to no name, cloaked in mystery, holding
secrets and answers only time will tell /

the months slip by quickly but the days are long /
soon there will be a chill in the air, yet most of my
memories in the season of change revolve around
warmth / ironic, isn't it? / how we recall what we
needed, not what was / or perhaps what we received
is more significant than the reason why /

the sun stumbles across the sky / peaks of orange
and pink rise up into the clouds / and i can feel
the changes in the air, autumn slowly beginning to
embed itself in my lungs / goodbye for now, sweet
summer sun. //

Sweeping the Floor

Reality settles in,
a coat too heavy for some to bear
A chain so flashy
only the most bold of us
would wear

The important things,
they are dishes
sitting forgotten in the sink
and the nonsense,
it consumes us
we'll always choose
the latter,
passing on the opportunity
to think

Love is a rug
collecting dust
like an obsessive reader
collects books,
they pile up and pile up
until you can't quite
remember
how the carpet looks

living proof

I don't want my life
to be an excuse
I made up for missing
a train
I should be aboard
I'm washing the dishes,
I'm sweeping the floor

a pair of shoes

I am growing into my life like a pair of shoes I bought when my toes were just a little shorter, ankles couldn't quite reach the back. / My feet would slip, now they are steady. / My heel is firm on the sole, my feet fit snug in the shoes / I have grown into my life in ways I wasn't sure I could do. //

Autumn is not just for dying things

The bitter aroma of decay settles in
as the exterior of trees shrivels and grays,
just imagine what's happening underneath.
I wonder if the roots are withering too;
if the falling leaves are just scratching the
surface of this ceremonious death.
Where Summer brought birdsong Fall
bears deep voids of silence.
The ease with which the season of changes
burns all the bridges built in the sunshine months
never fails to take my breath away.
But now my mother is baking a pie in the kitchen.
There are scarecrows at every other street corner.
The weather arrives each morning with a chill,
but somehow that makes the October sunsets
all the warmer. Tan lines have been replaced with
flannel shirts and boots. Head no longer
underwater, hair blowing in the wind.
Autumn is not just for dying things, I know that
now because I'm more alive than I've been.

living backwards

i've been trying to live
backwards
like a plant growing
downward instead of up
i am ready to look
towards the sun

Rabbit Hole of What Ifs

I am sewn together by
the rising sun, love,
& a little bit of stardust
but is that enough?
Lately, it feels like nothing is.
What if I'm not cut out
for this?
I keep wondering if any of
my dreams will come true
& what if they've changed?
Is it okay to shift gears & pursue
something my wide-eyed
younger self would never do?
Perhaps she would,
if she had gotten the chance to.
These days I'm learning
things I never knew,
what if this is my chance, too?

For every crooked line
I trace in the center of a tree
I discover another scar
on my right knee.
Is it okay to wonder, to wander
& still be figuring things out?
I'm only 17 but the years
are getting shorter & I still
can't seem to put my finger on
what my life is meant to be
about.

learning how to stand

summer has finally come to an end but the rain is
still coming, falling like april skies
yellow faded, like my tired eyes
what blossomed in spring is desolate now
what happened long ago is finally beginning to
come to an end somehow
the pockets of my corduroy warm the cold touch
of my hand
one bird calls to another somewhere out of sight
autumn is a broken leg, learning yet again
how to stand
oak trees welcome autumn like owls to the night
and now i think i finally understand

You too are nature

Feel the soil beneath your feet,
look up at the skies,
bask in the sun's heat
let the beauty overwhelm your eyes.
Run barefoot,
don't just taste but savor,
lie in the grass and when you reach
up to your hair to wipe away the soot
remember that you too are nature.

she will be back

that achingly sweet, smile so wide you can't help
but cry feeling, it's not a once in a lifetime thing.

happiness is no friend to solitude;
she will make her way back to you,
she will travel down the roads just as we do,
she will rejoin you and rejoice

that feeling, she will be back again
with a stronger voice
and a sweeter song
she hasn't forgotten where she belongs.

be ready for when she comes:
she will be soft and
vibrant as the rising sun,
making light of the desolate black.

and most of all
don't forget her,
she will be back.

lessons

if you don't learn the lesson the first time,
life will give you the chance to learn it again

life doesn't teach us, it gives us opportunities
to learn. remember this, my friend.

upstream

growing up is a salmon swimming against the tides / a deer caught in luminous headlights / growing up is fighting waters and wanting more / it is bolting headfirst into speeding traffic / it is the absence of second thoughts / it is a baby bird forgetting that is was only just born /

growing up is a salmon struggling against the tides / when you're in the lead, you can't see that there's anybody by your side / life knocks you *back back back* / no matter how hard you swim it pushes you off track / it gives you all it's got so that you're forced to give everything you've got too /

growing up is learning that red blood can look blue / it is the realization that war isn't just war, it is battle after battle after battle too / it is making peace with where you are / you are but a single star in a sky brimming with them like ants to a yard, like children to a park / but who's to say you're not the northern star? /

growing up is fighting your way upstream / it is waking up and losing sight of your dreams / it's all too much and it's all too soon / but then it always is, as assuredly as twelve o'clock comes at noon /

growing up is a salmon caught against the tides /
losing friends and switching sides / over awareness
of passing time / fighting the water because it's the
cycle of life /

i'm a salmon fighting my way upstream / rediscovering
old dreams / and getting lost in the currents along the
way / there is something to be said about losing one's
sense of direction / something to be gained, not in a
tangible sense / something more like a small ember of
introspection / sometimes as i swim the sun hits the
water in just the right time at the right angle / so that
i see myself in the blurred ripples and i think it is my
most accurate reflection /

growing up is learning it's not a matter of swimming
or sinking / it's about keeping your head up / letting
your body do what it knows to do when your mind's
all worn out from too much thinking / growing old
is fighting those same tides / the grooves are more
familiar / the waves don't scare you quite so much /
but it's the very same fight it always was //

four letters

what would become of this life if it weren't for the all encompassing tenderness which we hold steadfastly within this heart that beats & beats & beats against this sacred cage of bones? what would it be beating for at all? why do we speak, do we sing, do we inscribe meaning in the form of ink onto paper— what is language itself if only to omit that heartfelt, holy four letter word? what of the terror, the fright, the agony which we endure, what makes any of it worth putting up a fight? if it weren't for that four letter word, life would lose all meaning in an instant.

burn the evidence

burn any evidence that i exist.
i stand in tightly laced shoelaces
so that i mightn't trip.
sealed lips and
hands fall at my hips
conceal any attitude that may
persist
with bright-eyed benevolence.
the perfect picture of grace
and innocence,
bow down to his wit
with unclenched fists.
god forbid someone sees it.
i'll busy myself with boredom
and the alluring idea of a gentle kiss,
remain polite but avoid any possible
position of power.
don't take initiative
just sit
become familiar with my own silence,
after all, who am i to resist?
clench my fists,
hands on my hips,
nothing but a freckle adorning my wrist.
no earthly possessions belong to me
but my wit.
this body is nothing but an inheritance,
forgive my malevolence,
who am i to resist?
and if i should, burn the evidence.

she sat with herself

she sat with the silence long enough that it started
speaking
she sat with the pain long enough that it revealed its
source
she sat with her grief long enough that she felt its
origin in her heart
she sat with her problems long enough that they
walked away
she sat with herself and nothing changed

she listened to the silence only to find it's not as
quiet as she thought
she sat with her pain long enough that she
understood it
she sat with her grief until she learned that it was
love
she sat with her problems until she realized most of
them weren't problems at all
she sat with herself long enough that she could
finally stand tall

dreamer again

it's like i'm finally
a dreamer again
these wings have rested
for far too long
the sky is on the tip
of my tongue
& i sure did miss its taste
sunshine's warm embrace

it's like i've been
sleepwalking all this time
now i'm awake,
my eyes are wide

my gaze is firm
i don't know who i've
been for all this time,
but now i feel like
i'm finally me
and i've made up my mind
not to forget again
so easily

Pulsar Chaser

After Jocelyn Bell Burnell

The night skies are calling
reach out to that elusive
extended hand.
Comets & space dust
are falling
to the intangible where they
will land.

Look to the ether, look
to the paper
look through the lenses,
look where nobody else
has looked,
then look where everybody
else has looked—
your eyes are the game changer.
Nothing is static—
not even in the photographs
they took.

Look & look again
write until the muscles
in your hand are sore
& then write some more.

What some may write off
as interference or a glitch
could alter science as we
know it
in fact it just may be
revolutionary,
& they will hate to see
you be a revolutionary

but you will do it anyway
because you were born
to be a star gazer;
at the end of the day
you will always be a pulsar chaser.

Look Up *(a sonnet)*

The morning sun rises. Its presence does
not go ignored by a single plant or
songbird, or rabbit, but perhaps by a
few people, it goes unnoticed as they
go about their day. Looking at the ground,
colorless concrete, cracked in several
places beneath tired feet, some only
see the yellow lines and red street signs as
they turn corners and cross sidewalks, living
in a sliver of what this world has to
offer. They miss out on sunrises and the
good times, too worried about the goodbyes
staring down at the yellow lines they fail
to see the headlights as life passes by.

Trust

When I say, "things will turn out okay,"
I don't mean that everything will turn out
as you want it to. Life is not a fairytale & I don't
pretend it is, but I do believe that in the whole wide
universe you are right here for a reason, put a little
trust in that. You've got the strength and the wisdom
to handle whatever life might throw at you.
The truth is I have no clue what life has in store;
what I do know is you are capable of all of it,
so more than anything, put a lot of trust in yourself.

For Mother Earth

I want to be a good guest
I want to tread lightly
and leave my dirt outside.
Remove my shoes
and help clean up the dishes
because it's the least that I can do.
I want to bring everything
I've got to offer
to the table
and when it comes time
that I give up my seat
I won't linger, but breathe
my last breath
hoping with all my heart
that I have been a good guest.

poetry is dead

they say poetry is dead / but then tell me how its spirit has become entangled in my soul to no end / how my fingers feel most alive when they are scribbling poetry in pitch black ink / tell me how i'm pretty sure if you slit my veins you would see them flow in dark faulty verse / i'm almost certain it is my lifeline in every multiverse / if poetry is dead, why does it give me life? / consume my nights / tell me why writing is both my breath and my home / if poetry is dead, i must be a ghost //

tattooed in my mind

sometimes i wonder if it's a talent or a flaw
how quickly some people move on.
i've never been like that.
yesterday lingers on my mind
like a burnt tongue or a sore thumb.
there are constant reminders everywhere.
i can find people i love in everything;
street signs and favorite teas and square
dancing and passwords and journal entries
and the weather and chlorine and the scars
and the songs and the box of memories i keep
in my closet and the text messages i don't delete.

sometimes i wonder if it's a talent or a flaw
how quickly some people move on.
i'll never be like that. details tattooed
in my mind like words on paper,
like nostalgia to fall. i am a poet, after all.

meraki

Meraki is a word used in the Greek language to describe
scenarios when a person has really put a part of themselves
or their soul into something.

this gushing muscle of mine
is pouring onto the pages
red, red, read
watch it drip, drip, drift
into some semblance of language
bleed, bleed, believe
the crimson truth is all i have to offer
to you
i let it dry, i watch it stick
i call it poetry
but really it's got my whole heart
in it

life itself

live for nothing if not the joy of living itself / for the cool breezes and the hot summer sun / live for the deep conversations that come out of thin air and traveling into the pages of the books on your shelf / live for peeled oranges and ice cold tea / live for the sunsets and running fast, feeling free / live for midnights and all that they employ / and remember as you decide what to live for, if it weren't for sorrow there would be no joy //

one step at a time

we can only see so many feet ahead. trust the process darling, you will get there in the end. just take one step and one step again, that's all it takes. you don't have to see the destination right now to know that's where you're headed, my friend.

one of these days

one of these days you will forget
what you are crying for / it'll
happen slowly & then it'll hit you
all at once / i think that's what
healing is / the pain dissipates as
our bodies work to mend our
wounds / our minds take more
time to catch up, to recognize
that we're not bleeding anymore /
one of these days you will
remember what you made it this
far for / you used to be caught in
fight or flight, you don't have to
do either anymore //

the world didn't end

the world didn't end when i was 9
and afraid of the dark
the world didn't end when i was 10
and scared i would never leave my mark
the world didn't end when i was 11
and the years were passing too quick
the world didn't end when i was 12
and sick
the world didn't end when i was 13
and faced with the reality of growing up
the world didn't end when i was 14
and thought i'd never be enough
the world didn't end when i was 15
and almost lost it all
the world didn't end when i was 16
and never felt so small
the world didn't end every time i was
sure it would,
so what makes this time any different?
the world hasn't ended as i approach
adulthood
the world didn't end when i was a kid
the world didn't end so i stopped living
like it did

living room

the only life that i might save is my
own / that's why i mend my clothes &
make breakfast in the morning / i walk
in the sunlight & take the longer road / i
drink hot tea when the skies are storming /
i plant gardens & watch them bloom / i
am trying to recognize that of all the
houses i will live in, this body of mine
is my one true home / i am acting
accordingly, i am polishing the floors
& tidying the living room / i am
learning that the only life i might save is
my own. //

living proof *pt ii*

we're human
no railroads, no rusty engines
no instruction manual
no answers to this abyss of questions
you hold in the pit of your stomach
but isn't that the best of it?
we are akin to the caterpillar and her
metamorphosis. there is proof in the chrysalis,
snakeskin you shed, bruises in places you
once bled. there is proof in the naked truth
that you made it this far.
you are still standing wherever you are—
don't forget all the closed fists,
the nights that proved nightmares really do
exist, because they are also proof
that good dreams come out of dark nights, too.
we're just human, and this is just life;
excitingly, terrifyingly unknown
we walk on into the rest of it
darling, take my hand
let's make the best of it
dance with me in the rain,
we'll shed a few tears through the pain
if you can't see this naked truth,
look in the mirror, my friend,
for you are living proof.

Acknowledgements

Thank you to everyone who has shown me that nothing is impossible.

Thank you to my family, your endless support never fails to amaze me and I don't think I'll ever be able to express the full extent of my gratitude. I adore you all. This book would not exist without your love and support, nor would I.

Thank you to Taylor, the best editor I could possibly ask for. Thank you for seeing this book in its earlier stages and helping me make it the best that I could.

Thank you to Kyra, the best designer there is. Thank you for seeing my vision and for your brilliant creativity that made this book look more beautiful than I ever imagined.

Thank you to my parents for your unwavering support and encouragement, it is the reason for all of this.

Thank you to my grandparents, you inspire me every single day.

Thank you to Mari for being the best friend that I could ask for.

Reese Lieberman

Thank you to the Instagram writing community for showing me that there is a place for my words. I am grateful for every one of you. Thank you especially to Gabrielle, Purva, Dhanya, and Evan.

Last but not least, thank you dear reader, for dancing in the rain with me.

About the author

Reese Lieberman is a writer, dreamer, and lover of words. She self-published her first collection of poetry, *this world from my 2 eyez*, at fifteen years old and her subsequent volume, *Unmistakably Human*, at sixteen. She adores getting lost in the pages of a book, long walks, and hot cups of tea. She strives to find the beauty in this world, and share it through her poetry.

You can find her at @reesewith3e.s on Instagram, YouTube, and TikTok.

If you have any questions about the poems in this book, my writing process, or anything else contact me on Instagram, I would love to hear from you!